WARSAW

THE CITY AT A GLANCE

Stare Miasto
The Old Town is
amazing architec
brick by brick afte
a UNESCO World H

Metropolitan
Lord Foster's doughn
is sensitive to the are
while also being a thor   ..., modern,
eye-catching and tranquil public space.
See p066

Zachęta National Gallery of Art
A 19th-century urban palace housing
contemporary Polish and international
collections and a comprehensive art
and design bookshop.
See p030

Świętokrzyski Bridge
This cable-stayed bridge is a homage to
composer Frédéric Chopin and makes for
an illuminating journey at night.
See p013

Palace of Culture and Science
Loved and hated in equal measure, Stalin's
gift to the people of Warsaw is a conspicuous
beacon on the city skyline, while the area
around it is up for development.
See p012

Polonia Palace Hotel
This Beaux Arts hotel, opened in 1913, was
one of only a handful of buildings in the city
centre to survive WWII. It is renowned for
its cosmopolitan buffet breakfast.
See p022

WARSAW

THE CHANGING FACE OF THE URBAN SCENE

Warsaw conjures up images of an ugly, grey city, pockmarked with Soviet-era concrete tower blocks, but it's a reputation that it doesn't deserve. Few places have suffered like the Polish capital has. It has been devastated more times than it would prefer to remember, most recently during WWII, when a staggering 85 per cent of the city was destroyed. The dignified Poles responded by rebuilding the Old Town brick by brick, and were justly rewarded when the site was awarded UNESCO World Heritage status.

With so much land available after the war, coupled with the reconstruction policies of the 1950s-era Communist government, it's not surprising that there is so much good architecture from this period. What is sad is that much of it is being neglected. But, while many of these gems are being replaced by soulless skyscrapers and malls, it's good to see Polish-born architects, like Daniel Libeskind, and international architects, such as Lord Foster and Skidmore, Owings & Merrill, injecting some character into the city centre.

With such a tragic history, Varsovians have come to believe that their city is not worthy of being seen, and can be very mistrustful of tourists. And yet they have been through too much not to be also very proud of the place. It's all in the approach. Ask a local what there is to see in Warsaw and they'll tell you there is nothing. Tell them you don't think there's much to do and they can't wait to tell you all the great things you mustn't miss.

ESSENTIAL INFO

FACTS, FIGURES AND USEFUL ADDRESSES

TOURIST OFFICE
City of Warsaw Information Office
Aleje Jerozolimskie 54
T 22 474 1142
www.warsawtour.pl

TRANSPORT
Car hire
Avis
T 22 630 7312
www.avis.com
Taxis
Ursyn Taxi
T 22 9466
MPT Taxi
T 22 1919
Trains
Central Station
Aleje Jerozolimskie 54
T 22 9436

EMERGENCY SERVICES
Ambulance
T 999
Fire
T 998
Police
T 997
24-hour pharmacy
Nawilczej
Ulica Wilcza 21
T 22 622 8971

EMBASSIES
British Embassy
Aleje Róż 1
T 22 311 0000
www.britishembassy.pl
US Embassy
Aleje Ujazdowskie 29-31
T 22 504 2000
poland.usembassy.gov

MONEY
American Express
Krakowskie Przedmieście 11
T 22 635 2002
travel.americanexpress.com

POSTAL SERVICES
Post Office
Ulica Świętokrzyska 31-33
T 22 505 3316
Shipping
UPS
T 22 534 0000
www.ups.com

BOOK
Warsaw by David Crowley
(Reaktion Books)

WEBSITES
Architecture
www.architektura-murator.pl
Arts/Culture
www.polishculture.org.uk
Magazines
www.warsawvoice.pl
www.what-where-when.pl
Newspaper
www.gazetawyborcza.pl

COST OF LIVING
Taxi from Fryderyka Chopina Airport to city centre
£6.40
Cappuccino
£1.30
Packet of cigarettes
£1.20
Daily newspaper
£0.25
Bottle of champagne
£65

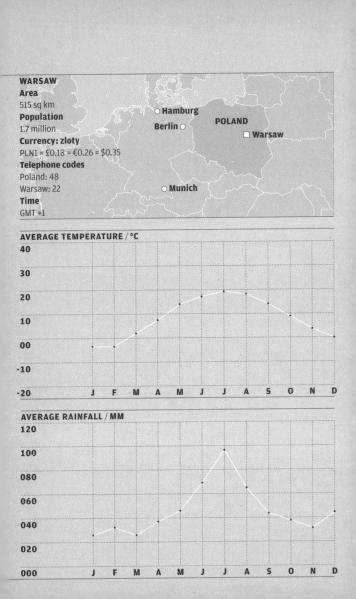

WARSAW
Area
515 sq km
Population
1.7 million
Currency: zloty
PLN1 = £0.18 = €0.26 = $0.35
Telephone codes
Poland: 48
Warsaw: 22
Time
GMT +1

Hamburg
Berlin
POLAND
Warsaw
Munich

AVERAGE TEMPERATURE / °C

40
30
20
10
00
-10
-20

J F M A M J J A S O N D

AVERAGE RAINFALL / MM

120
100
080
060
040
020
000

J F M A M J J A S O N D

NEIGHBOURHOODS
THE AREAS YOU NEED TO KNOW AND WHY

To help you navigate the city, we've chosen the most interesting districts (see below and the map inside the back cover) and colour-coded our featured venues, according to their location; those venues that are outside these areas are not coloured.

WOLA

This former working-class neighbourhood is fast becoming the financial district, with office blocks springing up in between old factories and tenements. Remnants of the former ghetto can be seen in the east, while the outdoor weekend Koło Bazaar (see p073) is great for bargains.

MOKOTÓW

Due to its combination of compact housing and numerous green areas, this buzzy district has a small-town intimacy but plenty of urban life in the form of cinemas, cafés, bars and restaurants. The area is particularly popular with creatives, who snap up the modernist apartments near Puławska and Madalińskiego.

ŻOLIBORZ

One of the city's two modernist districts, Żoliborz was largely built in the 1920s and 1930s. The wide streets, leafy parks and squares make this sleepy suburb a tranquil place to stroll. It's also the site of one of Europe's most architecturally stunning metro stations, Plac Wilsona (see p064).

POWIŚLE

Thanks largely to the University Library (see p010), this once-impoverished area has undergone a revival. New café/bookstores, such as Czuły Barbarzyńca (see p040) and Kafka (see p034), and the construction of smart apartment blocks have led to an influx of hip middle-class residents.

PRAGA

As one of the few districts to survive WWII almost intact, Praga is how the city once looked. Rundown and poor, it has been considered a dangerous neighbourhood in the past, but is now enjoying a renaissance, thanks to the large artist population and burgeoning hip bar and club scene.

STARE MIASTO/NOWE MIASTO

Literally meaning Old Town/New Town, much of this district was reconstructed from scratch after being reduced to rubble in the war. Hence Warsaw's historic centre feels quite detached from the rest of the city and not unlike a movie set. It's well worth visiting, however, to see its cobbled streets and mock-historical sgraffito.

ŚRÓDMIEŚCIE

The city centre is dominated by the iconic Palace of Culture and Science (see p012), and the brutal modernism of the BGK Bank (Aleje Jerozolimskie 7) and the former Communist Party HQ (Aleje Jerozolimskie/ Ulica Nowy Świat). Nightlife centres around Foksal, Jasna and Plac Trzech Krzyży.

SASKA KĘPA

Leafy streets and quaint corner stores give the city's other modernist district a village feel that makes it one of Warsaw's most expensive property areas. It's also home to numerous embassies, a large expat community, and the Stadion Dziesięciolecia (see p056), a vast stadium built in 1955.

LANDMARKS
THE SHAPE OF THE CITY SKYLINE

In the 1990s, Warsaw was the second largest building site in Europe (after Berlin). The various postwar planning committees could have let a spanking new city rise from the ashes, but instead they decided that to restore and recreate the architectural past was as necessary to wounded pride as building anew. Thus, 21st-century Warsaw's skyline features a mix of palaces, government buildings and glass and steel skyscrapers, though a close examination of the panoramic diagrams on the viewing platform of the Palace of Culture and Science (see p012) serves as a reminder that this city is changing faster than most. The Palace, which was finished in 1955 and originally intended to house the Communist Party HQ, is still Warsaw's most iconic and prominent landmark, although the InterContinental hotel (see p023) and RTKL's Warsaw Trade Tower (Ulica Chłodna 51, T 22 528 2222) are just two of a spate of modern skyscrapers redefining the city centre aesthetic.

Although most buildings turn their backs on the river, Warsaw University Library (see p010) and Świętokrzyski Bridge (see p013) have injected new life into the bankside Powiśle district. However, the most impressive landmark looks 16th century but was, in fact, completed in 1962. No visitor should miss a stroll through the cobbled streets and market squares of the Old Town, which was rebuilt using Canaletto's paintings of the city as reference.

For full addresses, see Resources.

Warsaw University Library
If ever there were an inducement
to study, it is Warsaw University's
reinforced concrete and glass library,
designed by Zbigniew Badowski and
Marek Budzyński and completed in
2000. Only students can enter this
lofty space, but visitors can enjoy the
inscribed copper-plate façade and
the stunning 2,000 sq m roof garden.
Ulica Dobra 56-66, T 22 552 5660

Palace of Culture and Science

It can be perplexing to hear Varsovians voice their hatred of this monumental Gotham City-esque skyscraper, designed by Russian architect Lev Rudnev and completed in 1955, but it's a little easier to understand when you know that it was a gift from Stalin. At the moment, the site around it is scrappy and lined with car parks and cheap supermarkets, but plans to redevelop the area, including building the much hyped Museum of Modern Art, should help redeem it to locals. Despite skyscrapers going up around it at a rate of knots, the 230m-tall tower is still a conspicuous beacon. It houses a viewing platform on the 30th floor, several cool bars, a fantastically nerdy technology museum and, if you delve deep enough, some lovely examples of 1950s interiors.
Plac Defilad 1, T 22 656 7723, www.pkin.pl

Świętokrzyski Bridge

Poland's first cable-stayed bridge when it was completed in 2000, the four-lane, 448m-long, asymmetric Świętokrzyski Bridge brings cars, cyclists and pedestrians across the Vistula river into the centre of the city from old Praga. A collaboration between Finnish bridge builder Mestra Engineering and local consultant BAKS, it features a single central 87.5m-tall A-type concrete pylon, topped with a black cover plate. This is intended to resemble a piano key, in homage to Polish composer Chopin. During the day, the bridge's white harp-like cables offer a navigational landmark, but it's at night, when it is illuminated and you're speeding over it in a taxi, that the bridge is at its most spectacular.

Warsaw Central Station

The main station has Leonid Brezhnev to thank for its completion. The design was subject to many revisions over a period of more than 20 years, before being hastily finished in 1975, in time for a visit by the Soviet premier. Designed by Arseniusz Romanowicz, it was hailed as a marvel of modernity when it opened, but, over the last 30 years, it has been neither renovated nor respected, and is now number two in the list of buildings Varsovians love to hate – the Palace of Culture and Science (see p012) holds the top spot. Sadly, it may be pulled down and replaced very soon. During the 1950s and 60s, Romanowicz also designed several smaller stations around Warsaw, including Śródmieście, Ochota, Powiśle and Stadion, which have all since acquired cult status.
Aleje Jerozolimskie 54

HOTELS

WHERE TO STAY AND WHICH ROOMS TO BOOK

A steady rise in capitalist enterprise since 1989, coupled with Poland's entry into the EU in 2004, means business in the city is booming. Sadly, this also means the Polish capital now sports a plethora of homogeneous chain hotels catering for the business market. The best of the bunch is the InterContinental (see p023), a one-legged landmark skyscraper with an excellent gym and pool (see p094). What Warsaw lacks are independent hotels aimed at the design-savvy tourist; the boutique-hotel scene was finally kick-started in 2003 with the art deco-inspired Rialto (see p020), and the contemporary Le Régina (see p018) opened the following year on a quiet cobbled street in the New Town.

Built in 1899, and close to the Old Town, Le Royal Méridien Bristol (Krakowskie Przedmieście 42-44, T 22 551 1000) is no newcomer, but its glamour had faded. Renovations and a recent acquisition by Starwood have put it back on the glitterati's radar. It's a similar story with the centrally located Polonia Palace Hotel (see p022), which was given a facelift in 2005. The Europejski (Ulica Tokarzewskiego) is a much mourned loss. It stopped functioning as a hotel in 2006, but you can still view the amazing lobby, designed in 1950 by Bohdan Pniewski, the architect responsible for the interiors of the Wielki Theatre (Plac Teatralny 1, T 22 692 0200) and the Sejm (see p068).

For full addresses and room rates, see Resources.

Residence Diana

Diana is all about home comforts. Opened in 2005 by Orco, the owner of Le Régina (see p018), this is less a hotel and more a block of serviced one- and two-bedroom apartments. Located in a mews close to the main tourist drag, Nowy Świat, it has interiors by UK firm Jestico + Whiles, who designed One Aldwych and the revamped Fortnum & Mason in London. Apartments are entered via a luminous lobby (above), and are equipped with high-tech kitchens, wi-fi, plasma-screen TVs, jacuzzis and balconies. Guests will appreciate the central yet quiet location, use of the spa facilities at Le Régina and underground parking. Some of the furnishings are a bit too Ikea, but the apartments are spacious, with the best being the split-level 510. *Ulica Chmielna 13a, T 22 505 9100, www.mamaison.com/warsaw*

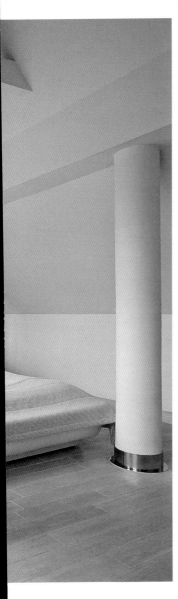

Le Régina

This luxury hotel opened in 2004, and it's still pretty shiny. Tucked away on a cobbled street in Nowe Miasto, on the site of the first US embassy, the renovated 18th-century building looks more like a 21st-century monastery, and is just as tranquil. French owner Orco insisted on special touches, such as the Louvre-esque glass pyramid in the central courtyard, which makes a romantic dining spot. The 61 rooms feature dark woods, Brazilian sandstone and hand-painted frescoes by Polish artist Anna Pabisiak. Ask for one of the Deluxe terrace rooms on the third floor, which have wooden floors, skylights and terraces overlooking the courtyard, or splash out on the Penthouse Suite (left). Sporting a different look to the rest of the rooms, its 1980s brashness makes it popular for photo shoots.
Ulica Kościelna 12, T 22 531 6000, www.leregina.com

Rialto

Designed by local firm DOM Architektury, this deco delight manages to be both elegant and cosy, and the Rialto is still the city's best boutique hotel option. The furniture is a mix of original 1920s pieces, as seen in the lobby (right), and locally handcrafted new ones, and the walls are adorned with vintage prints. Nice touches include the Bakelite light switches and 1920s-style air-conditioning units. All the rooms are individually decorated and come with a separate shower and roll-top bath; we think Room 57, the Rennie Mackintosh Suite, and Room 58 (above) are two of the dandiest. Charming staff, use of the exclusive Sinnet Club (see p094) and a restaurant (T 22 584 8771) run by Kurt Scheller, a Swiss-born local celebrity with a passion for Dalí, make a stay here a real pleasure.
Ulica Wilcza 73, T 22 584 8700, www.hotelrialto.pl

Polonia Palace Hotel

When this hotel, built in a Beaux-Arts style, opened in 1913, it was billed as 'very modern with hot and cold running water', and its distinguished guests have included Charles de Gaulle and General Eisenhower. It was one of only a few buildings in the city centre to survive WWII, but during communist times it became somewhat lacklustre – until a £20m facelift in 2005 transformed it into a smart hotel with a huge glass-roofed lobby. The 206 rooms are spacious, but the best ones are the five Junior Suites (above). We challenge anyone not to be impressed by the buffet breakfast, an eclectic smorgasbord that includes spring rolls, dim sum, Parma ham, French cheeses, caviar and – should you need a pick-me-up – vodka shots.
Aleje Jerozolimskie 45, T 22 318 2800, www.syrena.com.pl

InterContinental

This hotel's status as a Warsaw landmark was sealed when neighbouring residents complained that a skyscraper would block out their light. So, Polish architect Tadeusz Spychała cut part of the planned tower away to form a separate leg, and sliced a stone razor blade through the building from top to bottom, giving the hotel a unique shape that has proved a crowd-pleaser. The pool (see p094) and fitness area on the 43rd and 44th floors are also a draw. Double-height windows offer fantastic views of the neighbouring Palace. Book yourself into a corner suite – some have windows in the bathroom so you can groom with a view. Shopaholics should feel soothed by another attention-grabber next door, the Złote Tarasy mall (see p063). *Ulica Emilii Plater 49, T 22 328 8888, www.warsaw.intercontinental.com*

24 HOURS
SEE THE BEST OF THE CITY IN JUST ONE DAY

Warsaw is not large and taxis are inexpensive, so you can cover a lot of ground easily. Clearly, no trip would be complete without visiting the Palace of Culture and Science (see p012) or having a stroll and a coffee in Stare Miasto. However, the day outlined here will ensure you see as much of Warsaw, old and new, as possible. Start with a healthy breakfast and a healthy sprinkling of socialist-realist architecture at Café 6/12 (opposite), on a quiet street close to the busy Charles de Gaulle roundabout, then hail your first taxi of the day and head 10km south to Wilanów. This peaceful district is home to the 17th-century Wilanów Palace, dubbed the 'Polish Versailles', and a 45ha park (www.wilanow-palac.art.pl). While in the area, check out the stunning collection at the Wilanów Poster Museum (see p026), one of the city's highlights.

Catch a taxi back to the city centre to re-energise at Asian eaterie Sense (see p028). From here, walk east to Fotoplastikon (Aleje Jerozolimskie 51, T 22 625 3552), an original wooden peepshow that's been on this same spot, hidden down a dark alley, since 1905. Then take a jump from the past to the future of Polish art with a look around the Foksal Foundation Gallery (Górskiego Wojciecha 1a, T 22 826 5081) and the Zachęta gallery (see p030). Finally, catch a taxi to the decadent Belvedere (see p031) for dinner, before dancing until dawn at Utopia (Ulica Jasna 1, T 22 827 1540).
For full addresses, see Resources.

09.00 Café 6/12

It was the tall, willow-green concrete columns, marble floor and modernist chandeliers – original relics from its 1950s days as the offices of the national rubber industry – that first tempted us in, but it's the 76 types of smoothies that keep luring us back. Whether you have a vodka hangover or just feel in need of a tonic, there's a juice to fix it, with ingredients ranging from prunes and sesame seeds to cardamom. The food menu is equally expansive, so allow yourself plenty of time to peruse it, as well as the eclectic habitués. In recent visits, between the potted palms we've spotted glam couples lounging over breakfast, businessmen downing vodka shots with lunch, and twentysomethings mellowing out with monster lattes.
Ulica Żurawia 6-12, T 22 622 5333

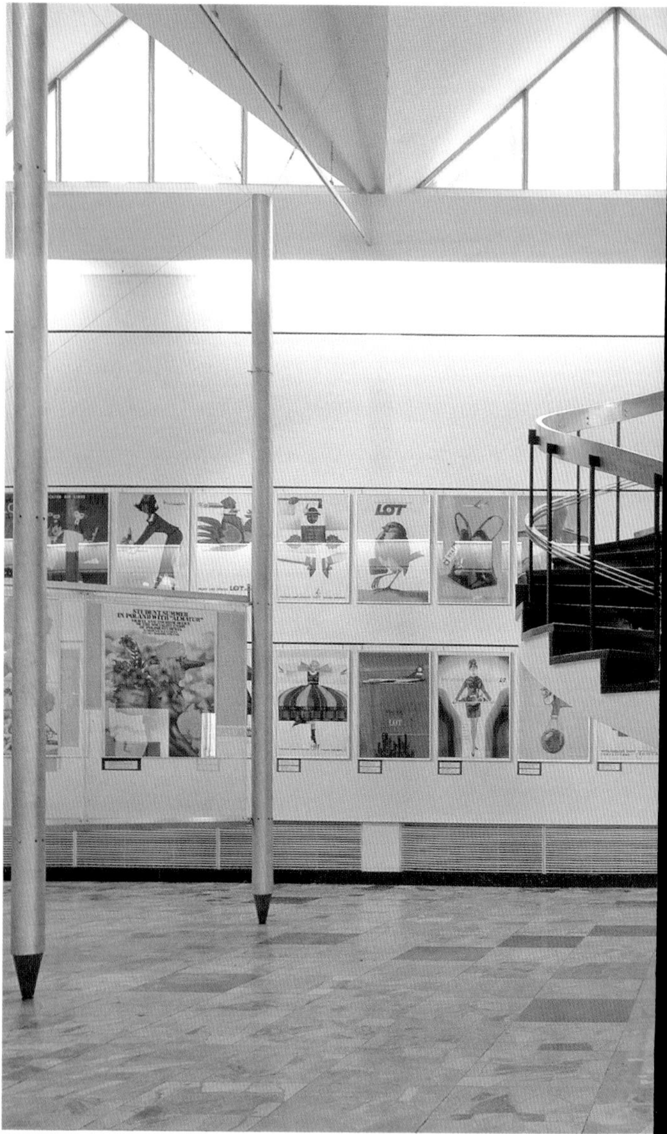
LOT
STUDENT SUMMER
IN POLAND WITH "ALMATUR"

12.00 Wilanów Poster Museum
No one designs posters quite like
the Polish, so it seems only fitting that
the country should have a museum
dedicated to this art. Boasting one of
the largest collections of posters in the
world, it includes works by Wiktor Gorka,
Jan Lenica and Tadeusz Gronowski, as
well as Dalí, Warhol, Picasso and Miró.
*Ulica St Kostki Potockiego 10-16,
T 22 842 4848, www.postermuseum.pl*

14.00 Sense

Some say this Asian fusion restaurant and cocktail bar has gone downhill since the original owner, Polish actress Katarzyna Figura, who also owns KOM (see p046), sold it, but on our visits it didn't seem that the numbers or the food had suffered. A Zen interior and a menu with wholesome options make this a good place if you feel you've been overdoing it, though we found ourselves repeatedly ordering the same thing: tempura fish and chips with green pea purée, strawberry lime lasagne and a Warsaw Waltz (Belvedere vodka, cranberry juice, fresh strawberries and lime). And if vodka is your thing, the bar has made a spirited attempt to have the biggest selection in the world, with 115 different types on offer, all served at a crisp -18°C. Service by staff in pyjama-like uniforms (a current trend in Warsaw) is spot on. *Ulica Nowy Świat 19, T 22 826 6570, www.sensecafe.com.pl*

16.30 Zachęta National Gallery of Art
One of the few city-centre buildings to survive the destruction of WWII, this 19th-century urban palace now dedicates itself to promoting contemporary Polish and international art. For a recent exhibition on Polish painting of the 21st century, this involved heavily splattering the grand staircase (above), Pollock-style, with primary-coloured paint. The gallery also has a comprehensive bookshop, with titles in Polish and English, and, for those who don't make it to Wilanów (see p026), a selection of catalogues from past poster biennales. Opposite the Presidential Palace (Krakowskie Przedmieście 46-48) just around the corner, the Zachęta's talented offspring, the Kordegarda Gallery (T 22 421 0125), continues the good work.
Plac Małachowskiego 3, T 22 827 5854, www.zacheta.art.pl

20.00 Belvedere

If time allows, grab a pre-prandial drink at hip café/bar/gallery and all-day hangout Między Nami (see p048) before you dine at the impossibly romantic Belvedere restaurant in Łazienki Park. This hothouse flower has been here for 15 years and has stood the test of time due to the owner's love of constant reinvention. The Asian-influenced interior, by opera-set designer Boris Kudlička, is a decadent arrangement of tropical foliage, black and gold lacquer chairs and red screens. Come here for a celebration with a group of friends, sitting at one of the large tables that run the length of the triple-height glass window, or take a date and dine on blinis with black caviar in a private alcove nestled discreetly among the exotic plants. *Łazienki Park (entrance on Ulica Parkowa), T 22 841 2250, www.belvedere.com.pl*

URBAN LIFE

CAFÉS, RESTAURANTS, BARS AND NIGHTCLUBS

The days of the milk bar serving up cabbage and dumplings on every street are long gone. Those with an appetite for communist-era dining could pull up a pew at Bar Ząbkowska (Ulica Ząbkowska 2, T 22 619 1388), one of only a handful of milk bars left, but the restaurant scene has moved considerably upmarket since then.

Of course, upmarket doesn't always equate to good taste, and minimalism is a rare word in the vocabulary of the Polish interior designer. This is never more evident than at the city's hottest foodie spot, AleGloria (Plac Trzech Krzyży 3, T 22 584 7080), an explosion of strawberry prints and plastic geese that shows not all kitsch is good kitsch. It belongs to the Gessler family, a dynasty of restaurateurs who also own the more sophisticated U Kucharzy (see p038). The traditional Polish fare served here is generally quite rich and hearty, so you might instead want to join in with Warsaw's current passion for Asian food, at Papaya (see p036), Sense (see p028) or the sushi café Skorupka (see p039).

In the chilly winter months, Varsovians cosy up with a good book and a latte at one of the city's many café/bookshops, such as Czuły Barbarzyńca (see p040), while in summer they descend on the riverbank beer gardens to enjoy live music. But all year round they love to go clubbing, with most venues kicking off around 3am and closing only when the last person leaves.

For full addresses, see Resources.

Foksal 19

The appeal of this haunt, loved by affluent Varsovian thirtysomethings, shows no sign of waning. Housed in a 19th-century Gothic revival building on one of Warsaw's buzziest streets, the sexy interior of this élite establishment is dominated by a long glowing amber bar and a full-length Tamara de Lempicka mural, and features a brash palette of black and gold dotted with Philippe Starck 'Louis Ghost' chairs.

An interesting cocktail menu includes cranberry caipirinhas and a Kate Moss, a shake-up of watermelon liqueur, *crème de bananes* and Malibu that we just had to try. Like most nightspots in Warsaw, things don't hot up here until late; after 11pm, the action moves upstairs to the ultraviolet lights of the club.
Ulica Foksal 19, T 22 829 2955, www.foksal19.com

Kafka

Cafés with a bookshop (or is it bookshops with a café?) are where the smart kids are hanging out. And who can blame them when there are so many places to get literary with your latte? The cute Kafka café, near the university, features coloured pipes, huge windows, deer-antler hooks, a black ceiling peppered with cut-out clouds and a chessboard floor. Its great coffee, wide range of teas, hot and cold sandwiches, salads and cakes are a magnetic draw, while the deep sofas and ledgefuls of second-hand books mean you might still be there when it closes at 10pm. Also make sure that you bookmark Antykwariat (T 22 629 9929) in the city centre, which boasts a wide selection of secondhand guides, novels and maps. *Ulica Oboźna 3, T 22 826 0822, www.kafka.com.pl*

Papaya
This restaurant's clinically chic ground-floor interior, featuring white walls, 'Panton' chairs and waiters dressed like beauty technicians, contrasts starkly with its dark, seductive basement den lined with geisha prints. The menu is an exhaustive run through the cuisines of China, Thailand and Japan.
Ulica Foksal 16, T 22 826 1199,
www.papaya.waw.pl

U Kucharzy

Set up in the kitchens of the old Europejski Hotel by the Gessler family – the Conrans of Warsaw – this is the city's most talked-about restaurant. It's a black-and-white tiled affair with pale wood furniture, and offers up the full food-as-theatre experience. Half the restaurant features rows of bar-like tables arranged so that diners can watch what's going on in the open kitchen. The other half consists of a series of more private spaces to which the chefs bring a portable wooden cooking trolley to finish off dishes at your table. The service by the heavily tattooed cooks can be a little on the sloppy side, although this only adds to the drama of it all. The food is largely high-class Polish, with wild boar, herring and sausage featuring heavily.
Ulica Ossolińskich 7, T 22 213 3393, www.gessler.pl

Skorupka

This eaterie has none of the blinding white minimalism of your average sushi joint, the type of interior that can lead you to bolt your bento and skedaddle sharpish. Instead, Skorupka's green walls, black pendant lamps and red leather seats give the place a glamorous oriental feel, putting you in the mood for lingering and allowing you time to get to grips with your chopsticks. Cute wallpapered alcoves, vintage chairs and a rogues' gallery of couples keeping an eye on how much tempura and temaki you can devour all add to the experience. Within spitting distance of the Zachęta National Gallery of Art (see p030), Skorupka also does breakfast (not sushi), cakes and cocktails for those who cannot resist its charms. *Plac Dąbrowskiego 2-4, T 22 892 0689, www.sushi.skorupka.pl*

Czuły Barbarzyńca

This well-designed café/bookstore is near the Warsaw University Library (see p010) in Powiśle, which explains why its various levels are always packed with cool kids tapping away on their MacBooks and filling up on the great coffee, homemade sandwiches and cakes. And it's not only popular with students; we were hard-pushed to find someone who didn't name this corner spot with wi-fi as their favourite place to chill out. The bookstore has a carefully chosen stock of art and travel books, with about 200 titles in English, as well as a selection of design, literary and architecture magazines. Extroverts, meanwhile, will enjoy the cowhide swing near the entrance which, says owner Tomasz Brzozowksi, is there to offer 'an antidote to gravity'.

Ulica Dobra 31, T 22 826 3294,
www.czulybarbarzynca.pl

Mono Bar

Before the Mono Bar was the Mono Bar, it was Labo, an extremely popular club that packed in the beautiful people for about four years. Consequently, the new owners had a lot to live up to. Luckily, Mono has proved to be a colourful character that's more than holding its own on the busy club scene. The venue, housed in the 1960s Artists' Association building on Ulica Mazowiecka, retains many of its original features, including a stunning concrete staircase and parquet flooring, as well as being kitted out with 1960s furniture, potted ferns and walls painted in bright colours and psychedelic patterns by local artists. Sorry Ghettoblaster, on the last Saturday of every month, is currently one of Warsaw's best nights out.
Ulica Mazowiecka 11a, T 22 827 4557, www.monobar.pl

Qchnia Artystyczna

Ujazdowski Castle was built in the 1970s, but is a replica of the original 17th-century one that was burnt out by the Nazis in 1944. Perched on an escarpment, it now houses Warsaw's Centre for Contemporary Art (T 22 628 1271), which hosts temporary shows by Polish and international artists, and holds a notable permanent collection, including a Jenny Holzer installation. The castle also houses a whimsical restaurant,

Qchnia Artystyczna (meaning 'artistic kitchen'), which describes its menu as 'postmodern' and turns out creative interpretations of Polish classics. In summer, its open-air terraces, offering fine views over Łazienki Park's fountains, lakes and greenery, hum with artistic types discussing the latest exhibition. *Ujazdowski Castle, Aleje Ujazdowskie 6, T 22 625 7627, www.qchnia.pl*

Numery Litery

On a rather drab street in the city centre, the Numery Litery ('numbers and letters') café/bookshop caught our magpie eyes when we spotted its glittering crystal-and-lightbulb chandelier through the full-length window. Inside, our instincts proved spot on. The single central table, littered with design magazines and surrounded by coffee-coloured armchairs, is the perfect place to spend a long and lazy afternoon.

On either side of the table, shelves offer brain nourishment in the form of a savvy selection of books and magazines on architecture, art, design and interiors, while skilfully made coffees and a good selection of teas and cakes provide the real thing. A discreet back room (above) is the place to not be seen.
Ulica Wilcza 26, T 22 622 0560,
www.numerylitery.pl

KOM

For much of the last century, all of Poland's telecommunications were cabled through this building, including some of Churchill's conversations with Stalin. KOM's prewar function as a telephone exchange was a strong influence on its latest incarnation as a restaurant, bar and gentlemen's club, owned by Polish actress Katarzyna Figura and her American restaurateur husband Kai Schoenhals. The maze of rooms has many original period features, including telegraph machines, floor tiles and cable systems. The three ground-floor eateries serve fusion food and an exhaustive list of more than 220 wines, but the basement Telegraph Bar, fashioned from zinc, and the Connoisseur library, with its private humidors, are the places to be.
Ulica Zielna 37, T 22 338 6353, www.komunikat.net.pl

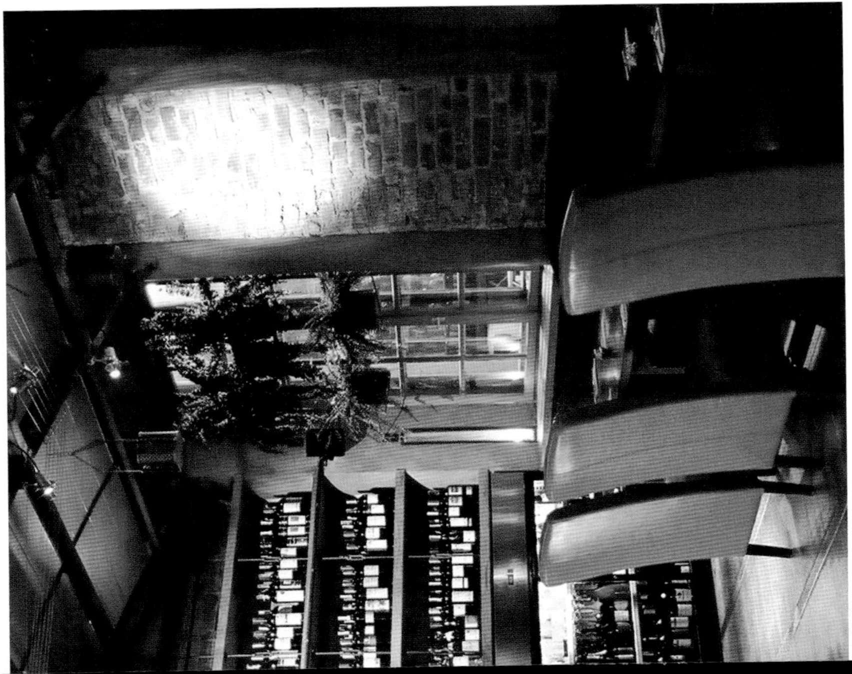

Między Nami

This perennially hip hangout can be hard to find as there's no sign outside, but it's long been a favourite with the media and fashionista crowd, who find the bare wooden floorboards and plain white concrete walls offer a blank canvas to show off their latest looks to best effect. The lofty two-storey café and restaurant doubles as a neat gallery space; on our visit there was a photography exhibition in collaboration with The Wapping Project for Jerwood. With aproned models earning extra zlotys serving up toasted sandwiches, soup and smoothies, it's worth dropping in to appreciate the whole landscape.
Ulica Bracka 20, T 22 828 5417,
www.miedzynamicafe.com

Platinium Club

Situated in a grand 19th-century building behind Saski Park, Platinium Club is the favourite haunt of sophisticated night owls. Not unlike a *Miami Vice* set, this spacious bar and supper club was the creation of renowned husband-and-wife design team Mirek and Iwona Kaczmarek. The main space features lofty columns, white leather sofas, chandeliers in red Perspex boxes, illuminated coloured glass dancefloors and big-name DJs, while a number of more private areas, such as the swirly patterned Mirror Room, offer conversation-friendly boltholes. Robert Pawelski, former head chef at Foksal 19 (see p033), rustles up supper dishes such as wild mushroom soup with crayfish tails and venison loin with cherry sauce.
Ulica Fredry 6, T 22 596 4666, www.platiniumclub.pl

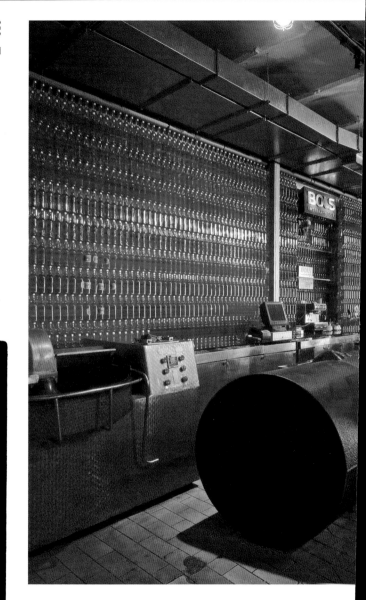

Fabryka Trzciny

Reminiscent of a scene from the film
Metropolis, this 2,000 sq m industrial
space, filled with machinery, iron girders
and pipes, is a haven for creatives. When
composer Wojciech Trzcinski first found
this former food-processing plant in 2001,
it was a derelict ruin coated in sludge. He
enlisted the help of Bogdan and Joanna
Kulczyński and Agnieszka Chmielewska to
transform it into a capacious media space.
An endless warren of rooms – some made
cosy by leather sofas, bookshelves and
chandeliers – offers a place to relax, drink
and eat, see live music, arthouse films,
exhibitions and lectures, and hold fashion
shows and photo shoots. It's a little off the
beaten track in Praga, but if you don't go,
you'll never get to see the illuminated
floor-to-ceiling bar (left) made of 4,000
bottles filled with purple liquid.
*Ulica Otwocka 14, T 22 619 0513,
www.fabrykatrzciny.pl*

Klub 55
One of the charms of the Palace of
Culture and Science (see p012) is that
there are so many hidden treasures
within its monumental walls – explore
its floors and you'll be rewarded. Klub
55 is one such find. Named after the
year the palace was completed, it's
one for insomniacs as the club doesn't
really kick off until about 3am.
Plac Defilad 1, www.klub55.pl

INSIDER'S GUIDE

ANIA KUCZYŃSKA, FASHION DESIGNER

After studying fashion in Rome and Paris, Ania Kuczyńska returned home to Warsaw eight years ago in order to start designing her first collection, and in 2006 she opened her own store (Ulica Solec 85, T 501 584 884). For a special night out, she books a table at U Kucharzy (see p038), where the chefs cook in front of the diners: 'I could sit for hours and watch them work,' says Kuczyńska. This would be followed by a trip over the river to M25 (Ulica Mińska 25, T 608 634 567), a club in a converted factory building in Praga, before heading to Klub 55 (see p052) in the early hours.

On quieter evenings, Kuczyńska will catch an old film by Fellini or Fritz Lang at the Iluzjon Cinema (Ulica Narbutta 50a, T 22 646 1260) near her home in Mokotów. If she feels like having a lazy afternoon, she'll pop into a gallery, such as Foksal Gallery (Ulica Foksal 1, T 22 827 6243) or Raster (Ulica Hoża 42, www.raster.art.pl), which resembles a big apartment. For good coffee in a welcoming atmosphere, she cosies up on one of the sofas in Czuły Barbarzyńca (see p040), which is a big favourite with the art and design set.

At weekends, Kuczyńska escapes the city; in winter this means heading off to Zakopane for a few days' skiing. She recommends the Kalatówki Mountain Hotel (Polona Kalatówki, T 18 206 3644). 'It's a bit basic, but it's so magical because it's perched on the slopes with nothing but woods and mountains around.'
For full addresses, see Resources.

ARCHITOUR

A GUIDE TO WARSAW'S ICONIC BUILDINGS

Warsaw is gradually filling the holes left by Russian occupation, communism and war. But, while buildings from the 16th and 17th centuries are still being reconstructed, little is being done to protect the city's late-modernist architecture. In December 2006, the Supersam supermarket, one of the most outstanding examples of postwar Polish architecture, was pulled down, while Stadion Dziesięciolecia (Ulica Targowa 33), designed in the 1950s, now houses one of the world's largest and seediest outdoor markets, and is earmarked for redevelopment. If these continue to be demolished to make way for the glass office blocks and bland shopping centres that have been sprouting since the fall of communism in 1989, Warsaw will lose some of its greatest assets.

It's not all bad. There has been a surge of new or improved embassies: the French Embassy (Ulica Piękna 1, T 22 529 3000), which was built in the 1960s with an envelope of portholed aluminium panels by Jean Prouvé, has been updated, while a new British Embassy is to be designed by Tony Fretton. Lord Foster's Metropolitan (see p066), completed in 2003, has brought purpose to a significant square with a troubled history, while the Museum of Modern Art, which will be the first project to break ground in the redevelopment of the area around the Palace of Culture and Science (see p012), should bring the city to the world's attention. *For full addresses, see Resources.*

Saska Kępa

Separated from the centre of Warsaw by the Vistula river, Saska Kępa is the more lively of the two modernist districts (the other, Żoliborz, is to the north). A largely unpopulated area before WWI, most of its buildings went up in the late 1920s and early 1930s, resulting in an avant-garde mixture typical of the interwar period. Start your architour with the modernist St Andrzeja Boboli church (overleaf) on

Ulica Nobla Alfreda. Designed by Józef Łowiński and Jan Bogusławski and completed in 1956, its yellow pipe-organ exterior opens up to reveal a latticed concrete ceiling and colourful murals. Then explore the prewar modernist villas and apartment blocks of this leafy enclave, focusing on Obrońców (above), Francuska and Katowicka streets, where you'll find heavily security-conscious examples.

St Andrzeja Boboli church

Agora building

Housing a magazine and newspaper group, this office block is a multi-layered lesson in how to look after your employees. When Agora commissioned local architectural firm JEMS Architekci, it said it wanted to encourage non-hierarchical contact and informal meetings. The result is a wonderfully egalitarian building (editors' offices are much the same as everyone else's) that manages to combine ecological awareness with innovative design. The façade is made up of glass and wooden shutters, punctuated by balconies and covered terraces, while work areas are arranged around a series of triple-height, glass-roofed atriums, drawing in daylight at every opportunity. Since being built in 2002, it has picked up a sackful of awards. *Ulica Czerska 8-10, T 22 555 6000, www.agora.pl*

Warsaw School of Economics

The SGH (Szkoła Główna Handlowa), or School of Economics, boasts some great examples of art deco and constructivist architecture. Three buildings were planned by architect Jan Koszczyc-Witkiewicz in the 1920s, but only two were built before WWII intervened. Koszczyc-Witkiewicz had his own style – a crossbreed of the so-called 'Polish national style', expressionism and constructivism. In fact, his aesthetics fitted in neatly with the social-realist doctrine later imposed by the Russians on Polish architecture after the war, so the remaining building was finished in 1954 to the original prewar design. The school is located over the Pole Mokotowskie metro station, and all the interiors are open to the public. *Aleje Niepodległości 162, T 22 564 6000, www.sgh.waw.pl*

Złote Tarasy

Sporting one of the largest glass roofs in the world, with more than 4,700 triangular panes of glass, the Złote Tarasy (Golden Terraces) shopping and entertainment centre opened in 2007. The complex, which also features three office buildings and a multiplex cinema, covers 225,000 sq m, making it one of the largest of its type in Europe. The concept was developed for ING Real Estate by LA-based architects

The Jerde Partnership, in collaboration with Polish firm Epstein, who liken the undulating roof to a silk shawl draped over billiard balls. Beneath this transparent masterpiece of engineering, escalators, with their mechanisms painted red and green and covered in glass panels, criss-cross between cascading terraces.
Ulica Złota 59, T 22 222 2200,
www.zlotetarasy.pl

Plac Wilsona metro station

The Warsaw metro, one of Europe's newest, opened in 1995 and consists of a single north-south line that is still partly under construction. Many of the stations are fairly ordinary to look at, but the Plac Wilsona station, serving the modernist suburb of Żoliborz, is something of an architectural masterpiece. Designed by Polish architect Andrzej Chołdzyński, and completed in 2005 at a cost of £16m, the platform features a central line of white reinforced-concrete trunks that branch into a wavy ceiling. Stairs lead up to the ticket level where, floating surreally above, is a flat, elliptic, black-ringed ceiling lit by fluorescent lamps that change colour depending on the weather, creating an atmosphere of serenity in an environment that is more traditionally associated with chaos and commotion.
Plac Wilsona, T 22 655 4000,
www.metro.waw.pl

Metropolitan
Lord Foster's solution for the missing
northern edge of Piłsudski Square is
a dignified doughnut-shaped building
that appears transparent when viewed
head on, yet solid from the side. The
central area, featuring a fountain, trees
and benches, is popular in summer, as
are the ground-level bars.
*Plac Piłsudskiego 1, T 22 820 2020,
www.metropolitan.waw.pl*

Sejm

One of the stars of Polish late modernism, Bohdan Pniewski is responsible for some of the city's most elegant postwar rebuilds. After the Wielki Theatre (T 22 692 0200) was bombed in 1939, he spent 20 years restoring its interiors. Hotel Europejski (see p084), damaged in 1944, also got the Pniewski modernist magic touch. In 1949, the Sejm, the seat of the lower house of the Polish parliament, endorsed a series of new buildings by Pniewski. Its entrance hall features his characteristic grey, black and white marble floors and white columns, while in the seat of the senate is a stunning free-standing oval staircase (above). Behind the Sejm, there's the chance to see Pniewski's former home, now housing part of the Museum of the Earth (T 22 629 8064).
Ulica Wiejska 4-8, www.sejm.gov.pl

Royal Netherlands Embassy
On the edge of Łazienki Park, the most eye-catching of the ambassadorial complexes is by Dutch architect Erick van Egeraat. The first thing you notice is the fence made of green steel shrubbery, in blissful harmony with the stark façade. Inside, Erwin Olaf's ceiling painting of faces is a wonderfully unorthodox touch.
Ulica Kawalerii 10, T 22 559 1200, www.nlembassy.pl

SHOPPING

THE BEST RETAIL THERAPY AND WHAT TO BUY

Even though Warsaw is a small city, the best places to shop are quite spread out, so unless you like everything under one roof – in which case head straight for the glass-bubbled world of Złote Tarasy (see p063) – be prepared to spend some of your zlotys on cab fares.

If furnishings are what you're after, the converted factory in the courtyard at Ulica Burakowska 5-7 houses the Vitra showroom (T 22 887 1064), while Idea + Forma (Ulica Duchnicka 3, T 22 322 5020) is a street away. Or cross the river to hip new district Praga for a browse in Magazyn Praga (overleaf). Looking for a stunning rug in an original modernist pattern? Tucked away in a car park on the edge of Łazienki Park, the ŁAD Royal Weaving Workshops (see p086) could make you one in a week.

Vodka is something the Polish have been making for centuries, and Ballantine's (see p077), in the city centre, is the best place to pick up a bottle. There are few things Poles love more than vodka, but one of them is chocolate. Wedel (see p076) has been feeding that particular addiction since 1851. Visit its fin-de-siècle parlour for hot chocolate, or to buy one of its beautiful bars.

If you're a sucker for design, you can't beat a poster as a keepsake. The archive exhibitions at the Wilanów Poster Museum (see p026) mean you can try before you buy, while original works have been spotted for sale at the Koło Bazaar (opposite).

For full addresses, see Resources.

Koło Bazaar

You might have to give up a night on the town to get the most out of Warsaw's best flea market, which is held around a square in the Wola district on Saturdays and Sundays. Although it doesn't wrap up until about 2pm, stalls set up at dawn, and by 11am it's mostly useless junk. Arrive early and you might be able to haggle for anything from modernist ceramics, art deco furniture and glass lamps to 1950s clocks, communist memorabilia and vintage posters by Polish artists, such as 'The Sea Days Celebration' by Wiktor Gorka (above). A number of posters were snapped up here by the owner of the Rialto (see p020) to display in the hotel.
Ulica Ciołka Erazma/Ulica Obozowa

Magazyn Praga
On returning to Poland from New York in 2006, art historian Łukasz Drgas set up this furniture store in a former vodka factory in cool, up-and-coming district Praga. His finds, including pieces by Polish designers such as Puff-Buff, are quickly snapped up by arty types. *Ulica Ząbkowska 27-31 (entrance on Ulica Markowska), T 22 670 1185, www.magazynpraga.pl*

Wedel Chocolate Parlour

Sweet-toothed Poles have been indulging in Wedel products since the factory started making chocolate back in 1851. In 1894, the company opened its Chocolate Parlour in a fin-de-siècle building on Ulica Szpitalna, where it still stands today. Its Regency-style parquet-floored tearoom serves creamy hot chocolate in white bone china teacups and a 'cacaophony' of desserts and cakes, while the shop features glass counters filled with beautifully packaged bars, cutely wrapped candies and unusual chocolate sculptures. The company's most famous product, however, is the Wedel Torte, a five-layer praline-filled round wafer that's dipped in dark chocolate and decorated by hand, meaning no two tortes are ever exactly the same.
Ulica Szpitalna 8, T 22 827 2916, www.wedel.pl

Vodka

Vodka shots by international companies such as Smirnoff and Absolut can be knocked back at every smart bar in town, but it seems only right to partake of the local hooch. There are lots of imitations, but for genuine Żubrówka (bison-grass vodka; above), look for bottles containing a blade of grass. Belvedere and Chopin, the only two vodka companies in the LVMH portfolio, are single-ingredient vodkas that make martinis we could drink all night. Meanwhile, architecture junkies should update their drinks cabinet with Wyborowa's Single Estate bottle, designed by Frank Gehry, who drew inspiration from his Polish heritage. Try Ballantine's (T 22 625 4832) for the perfect souvenir. Or, if you're not sure what you like, take a tour of the Koneser Vodka Factory (T 22 619 9021), which includes guided tastings.

Zoom

As the designers behind Vis à Vis, Anna Wojczyńska and Wojciech Wachowski have been the upholders of good furniture and product design in Warsaw for nearly 10 years. Their work has been shown at numerous international design and furniture fairs, with pieces such as their interactive 'Don't Think Just Play' lamps catching attention. As the owners of Zoom, the city's most intelligent furniture store, they champion global and local talent. The vast warehouse, located in an old printing factory, was a Vis à Vis design and also houses their studio on a mezzanine overlooking the shop floor. Their website asks new designers to send in pictures of ideas, which could get produced if good enough, with the latest outcome being a vinyl tablecloth featuring an aerial section of any part of Warsaw you like.
Ulica Nowogrodzka 84-86, T 22 816 2065, www.zoom.waw.pl

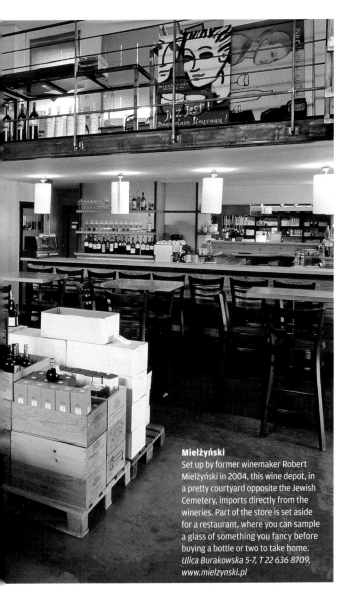

Mielżyński
Set up by former winemaker Robert
Mielżyński in 2004, this wine depot, in
a pretty courtyard opposite the Jewish
Cemetery, imports directly from the
wineries. Part of the store is set aside
for a restaurant, where you can sample
a glass of something you fancy before
buying a bottle or two to take home.
*Ulica Burakowska 5-7, T 22 636 8709,
www.mielzynski.pl*

Moho Design

Magda Lubińska and Michał Biernacki are
Poland's brightest design stars in more
ways than one. They set up Moho Design
in 2004 to produce beautifully made,
brightly coloured rugs using felt made
from pure New Zealand wool and inspired
by traditional Polish folk art. In 2005, they
went down a storm at 100% Design in
London, and in 2006 we gave them a
much-deserved Wallpaper* Design Award
for their 'Hej! Dia' rug (right). That year,
they also met industrial designer Ross
Lovegrove, who, charmed by their passion
and the unique results they were getting
with felt, collaborated with them on a
new rug collection, 'Laurasia', which was
launched in 2007 at the Milan Salone.
Got a floor that needs to make its impact
felt? Moho's rugs are available at Studio
Forma 96 (T 22 583 6858), Recamiere
(T 22 629 5085) and Vitra (see p072).
www.mohodesign.com

Galilu Neoperfumeria

When BBDO ad exec Agnieszka Łukasik and art buyer Wazynia Grela discovered that they had something else in common apart from employing the same interior designer – a mutual despair at the lack of good skin-pampering concoctions in Warsaw – they decided to set up shop on the ground floor of the former Hotel Europejski. They brought in architects Marcin Kwietowicz and Grażyna Czarnota, who retained many original 1950s features, such as a concrete spiral staircase, but added a modern baroque feel. Products by REN, Aesop, Malin+Goetz and 4mula line the backlit shelves, while a separate fragrance area features perfumes by Miller Harris. However, the colourful Claus Porto soaps are a clear winner.
Hotel Europejski, Krakowskie Przedmieście 13, T 22 828 3900, www.galilu.pl

ŁAD Royal Weaving Workshops

In a greenhouse in the car park of the Belvedere (see p031) are 12 original hand-operated 150-year-old Jacquard looms, weaving wool, linen and gold thread into bespoke tablecloths, rugs and curtains. There is a small collection of modernist patterns, including designs by leading 20th-century Polish artists. Allow a day per metre for items to order.
Łazienki Park (entrance on Ulica Parkowa)

SPORTS AND SPAS

WORK OUT, CHILL OUT OR JUST WATCH

The Poles love to watch football, and in particular the country's most successful side, Legia Warszawa, whose home ground is the interwar Polish Army Stadium (Ulica Łazienkowska 6). The Poles like a kick-about, too, but they love basketball more, and there are courts in every park and sports hall. One of the coolest places to shoot hoops is at the courts near the Wilanowska metro station (Aleje Wilanowska), where a number of tournaments are held, including freestyle and slam-dunk, often accompanied by DJ sets. If you want to watch a game, one of the city's best teams, Polonia Warszawa, sometimes plays in the sports hall at the modernist Akademia Wychowania Fizycznego (overleaf).

Eastern Europeans are hardly amateurs when it comes to the spa, treatment and fitness-centre game, and while Warsaw's hotels dominate the sophisticated options in this field, there are some good independents, such as Multico Wellness & Spa (see p092), and the diplomats' favourite, the Sinnet Club (see p094), a little out of town in Sadyba. The two activities the Polish élite enjoy more than any other, though, are equestrian sports and skiing. Throughout the winter months, Varsovians hit the Tatra Mountains for some on- and off-piste action. And when it's warmer, they saddle up one of their stabled stallions for a countryside canter or cheer on a chukka or two at the Buksza Polo Club (see p093).

For full addresses, see Resources.

Basketball

Ever since Polish television started broadcasting NBA games, basketball has taken off as the sport of choice for those looking to expend excess energy. All year round, the numerous basketball courts that have sprung up over Warsaw in the last 10 years are packed with amateur leagues bouncing balls and shouting a lot; in summer, matches played at the more spectacular outdoor venues often feature some kind of soundtrack. The six outdoor courts in front of the Palace of Culture and Science (above; see p012) are open daily until late, and you can watch games while bands play on nearby stages.

Akademia Wychowania Fizycznego

Also known as the AWF, the Academy of Physical Education is the largest in Poland, and one of the biggest in Europe. Built between 1928 and 1930 according to the plans of prominent Polish modernist architect Edgar Norwerth, this white concrete complex was designed in the Bauhaus style, incorporating traces of neoclassicism. In the 1960s, the academy was expanded to include an Olympic training centre designed by the architect and Olympic fencer Wojciech Zabłocki. Set in 79ha in the picturesque surrounds of the Bielany Forest in north Warsaw, the AWF's purpose is to educate teachers of physical education, but it also has a public sports and fitness centre so all can enjoy its architecture.
Ulica Marymoncka 34, T 22 834 0431, www.awf.edu.pl

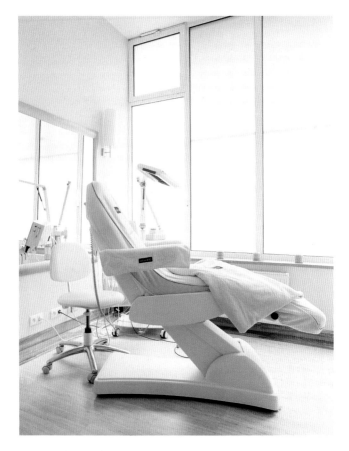

Dr Irena Eris Cosmetic Institute

Poland's answer to Estée Lauder, Dr Irena Eris is something of a legend among the pampered classes. The former pharmacist started her skincare brand in 1983 and weathered the difficult communist years to lead the Polish skincare market. She now has 30 salons worldwide, stocking her simple white jars and offering a portfolio that includes glycolic peels and endermology. Alternatively, head to wealthy Żoliborz to visit Multico Wellness & Spa (T 22 869 9631), which bases its treatments around the four elements of earth, fire, water and air. It offers a decent gym, yoga and Pilates classes, a steam room, a sauna and a mosaic-tiled 17m pool lined with glass doors that open out onto a plant-filled sun terrace.
Ulica Puławska 120-124, T 22 844 6567, www.drirenaeris.pl

Buksza Polo Club

Varsovians love to ride, and many wealthy kids stable horses. A brisk canter through the city's Łazienki Park can be an uplifting way to spend an afternoon – persuade the Cavallo Club (T 22 841 2250) to lend you one of its horses – or head a little out of town for a real hot-to-trot experience. The Buksza Polo Club is located less than an hour from Warsaw, yet surrounded by acres of virgin pine forest. It's where the élite gather at weekends to watch polo and enjoy Argentine barbecues, and it offers riding lessons and polo classes for those who fancy getting in on the chukka action themselves. It is also possible to book riding lessons at the Żurawno Polo Club (T 22 796 5358) and at Stajnia Chojnów (T 22 736 2878).
Ulica Obręb 32a, Góra Kalwaria, T 601 332 584, www.bukszapolo.pl

Hotel gyms

Gym connoisseurs should make sure their hotel booking is at the InterContinental (see p023), Rialto (see p020) or Hyatt Regency (T 22 558 1234). Cosily tucked away in the basement of the Hyatt, the Oasis Club (T 22 851 0563) combines the latest fitness technology with a Zen approach, offering a gym, heated pool, sauna, health bar and treatment rooms. Meanwhile, The Riverview Wellness

Centre (T 22 328 8640) prefers to hog the top two levels of the 44-floor InterConti, providing hotel guests with spectacular views while they lap the pool (above) or pound the Technogym treadmill. The Rialto has a nicely designed gym, steam room and sauna, but also offers its guests use of the exclusive members-only Sinnet Club (T 22 550 3400), much patronised by British Embassy staff.

ESCAPES

WHERE TO GO IF YOU WANT TO LEAVE TOWN

Warsaw experiences an extreme climate. In the snowy winter months, temperatures can plunge to -16°C, while at the height of summer they reach a sweltering 30°C, making escaping the city a way of life. In winter, this largely involves heading off to the cosy chalets around Zakopane, in the Tatra Mountains, where you can find some of the best skiing in central Europe. And when the stifling heat of summer hits, the smart set hit the beach, heading north to the fashionable spa resort of Sopot (see p100).

Ask Varsovians what there is to see in Warsaw and they will probably tell you that you're better off going to Krakow, generally considered to be Poland's cultural capital. In stark contrast to Warsaw, the city suffered almost no war damage and boasts a rich blend of Renaissance, baroque, Gothic and modern architecture. One of Poland's youngest cities is Łódź – the childhood home of architect Daniel Libeskind – which flourished in the 19th century as a centre of the textile industry. The old mills are now being given a new lease of life – Manufaktura (Ulica Ogrodowa/Ulica Zachodnia, T 042 664 9289) is a series of factories that have been transformed into Europe's largest shopping, entertainment and cultural centre. Architecture fans should journey further south to the Silesian cities of Katowice (opposite) and Bielsko-Biała to see some of the country's best modernist architecture.

For full addresses, see Resources.

Katowice

In the Silesian city of Katowice, Bauhaus-inspired buildings sit beside communist-era marvels, such as the UFO-like Spodek arena, and newer additions, including the angular Silesian Library (overleaf; Plac Rady Europy 1), completed in 1997. Among the city's gems is one of Europe's first skyscrapers, Drapacz Chmur (above; Ulica Żwirki i Wigury 15), designed by Tadeusz Kozłowski to house tax-office employees and completed in 1934. Close by is another beautiful example of functionalism, Leon Dietz d'Arma's 1930 St Kazimierz church (Ulica Kopernika). If you want to stay over, check in to the Hotel Monopol (T 032 782 8282), with its lush modernist interiors.

Sopot

When Varsovians want to beat the summer heat, they head north to the Polish Riviera and the chic seaside town of Sopot. About four hours away by train, the resort has been fashionable since the 19th century, with both aristocrats and artists attracted by the spa facilities and sea air. The town is awash with charming fin-de-siècle architecture, but really it's all about the water here. Sopot has the longest wooden pier in Europe and 4.5km of coast, dotted with clean, sandy beaches. This strip is shielded by the Hel Peninsula (where the beaches are even better), making the water the warmest in the Baltic. Stay at the Sofitel Grand hotel (T 058 520 6000), which has been restored to its original art deco splendour, or the Bryza Spa Hotel (T 058 675 5100) in Jurata.
www.sopot.pl

Kazimierz Dolny
Throughout summer, artists, musicians
and writers flock to this tiny historic town
on the banks of the Vistula to enjoy the
landscape and the numerous festivals,
outdoor film showings, art exhibitions
and concerts. The 115-room Hotel Król
Kazimierz (T 081 880 9999), which
is housed in a restored 17th-century
granary, regularly organises picnic tours
of the town and its lovely surroundings.

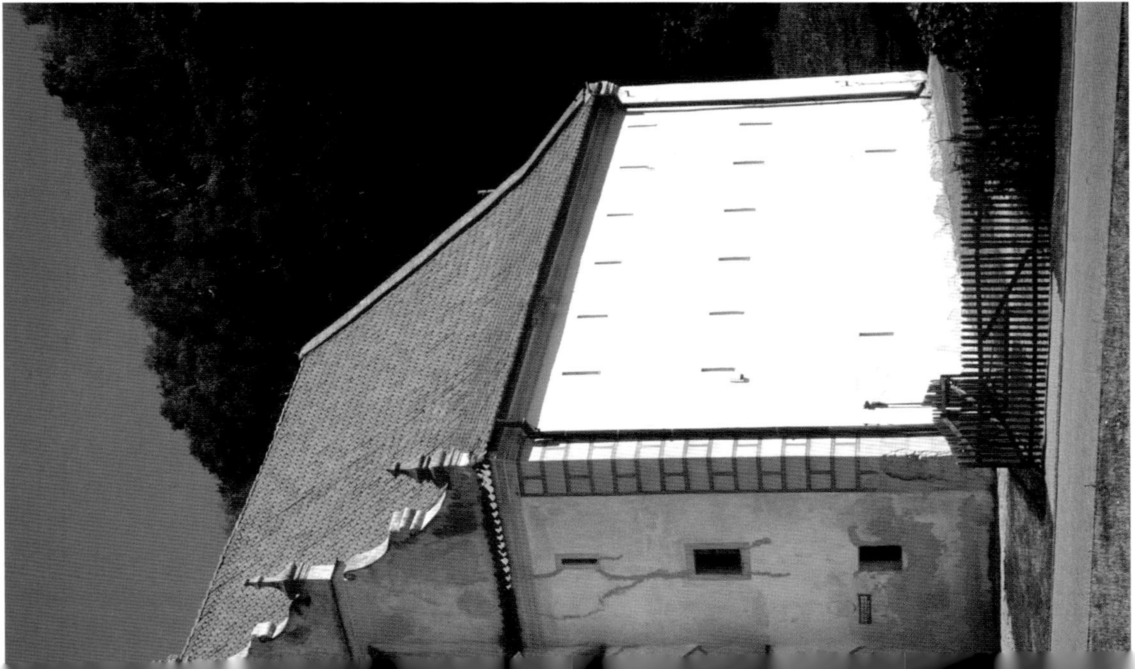

NOTES

SKETCHES AND MEMOS

RESOURCES
CITY GUIDE DIRECTORY

A

Agora building 060
  Ulica Czerska 8-10
  T 22 555 6000
  www.agora.pl
Akademia Wychowania Fizycznego 090
  Ulica Marymoncka 34
  T 22 834 0431
  www.awf.edu.pl
AleGloria 032
  Plac Trzech Krzyży 3
  T 22 584 7080
  www.alegloria.pl
Ania Kuczyńska 054
  Ulica Solec 85
  T 501 584 884
  www.aniakuczynska.com
Antykwariat 034
  Ulica Żurawia 45
  T 22 629 9929

B

Ballantine's 077
  Ulica Krucza 47a
  T 22 625 4832
  Ulica Puławska 22
  T 22 542 8622
  www.sklep-ballantines.pl
Bar Ząbkowska 032
  Ulica Ząbkowska 2
  T 22 619 1388
Belvedere 031
  Łazienki Park
  (entrance on Ulica Parkowa)
  T 22 841 2250
  www.belvedere.com.pl
Bryza Spa Hotel 100
  Ulica Międzymorse 2
  Jurata
  T 058 675 5100
  www.bryza.pl

Buksza Polo Club 093
  Ulica Obręb 32a
  Góra Kalwaria
  T 601 332 584
  www.bukszapolo.pl

C

Café 6/12 025
  Ulica Żurawia 6-12
  T 22 622 5333
Cavallo Club 093
  Ulica 29 Listopada 3a
  Łazienki Park
  T 22 841 2250
  www.belvedere.com.pl
Centre for Contemporary Art 043
  Ujazdowski Castle
  Aleje Ujazdowskie 6
  T 22 628 1271
  www.csw.pl
Czuły Barbarzyńca 040
  Ulica Dobra 31
  T 22 826 3294
  www.czulybarbarzynca.pl

D

Drapacz Chmur 097
  Ulica Żwirki i Wigury 15
  Katowice

F

Fabryka Trzciny 050
  Ulica Otwocka 14
  T 22 619 0513
  www.fabrykatrzciny.pl
Foksal Foundation Gallery 024
  Górskiego Wojciecha 1a
  T 22 826 5081
  www.fgf.com.pl

HOTELS
ADDRESSES AND ROOM RATES

InterContinental 023
Room rates:
double, from €100;
corner suite, €160
Ulica Emilii Plater 49
T 22 328 8888
www.warsaw.intercontinental.com

Polonia Palace Hotel 022
Room rates:
double, from €150;
Junior Suite, €190-€270
Aleje Jerozolimskie 45
T 22 318 2800
www.syrena.com.pl

Le Régina 018
Room rates:
double, from €120;
Deluxe, €250;
Penthouse Suite, €650
Ulica Kościelna 12
T 22 531 6000
www.leregina.com

Residence Diana 017
Room rates:
apartment, from €180;
Apartment 510, €360
Ulica Chmielna 13a
T 22 505 9100
www.mamaison.com/warsaw

Rialto 020
Room rates:
double, from €150;
Room 57, €220;
Room 58, €220
Ulica Wilcza 73
T 22 584 8700
www.hotelrialto.pl

Le Royal Méridien Bristol 016
Room rates:
double, from €279
Krakowskie Przedmieście 42-44
T 22 551 1000
www.warsaw.lemeridien.com

WALLPAPER* CITY GUIDES

Editorial Director
Richard Cook

Art Director
Loran Stosskopf
City Editor
Anne Soward
Editor
Rachael Moloney
Executive
Managing Editor
Jessica Firmin
Travel Bookings Editor
Sara Henrichs

Chief Designer
Daniel Shrimpton
Designer
Ingvild Sandal
Map Illustrator
Russell Bell

Photography Editor
Christopher Lands
Photography Assistant
Robin Key

Chief Sub-Editor
Jeremy Case
Sub-Editors
Vicky McGinlay
Stephen Patience
Assistant Sub-Editor
Milly Nolan
Interns
Chloe Fletcher
Ella Marshall
Lizzy Tinley

Wallpaper* Group
Editor-in-Chief
Tony Chambers
Publishing Director
Andrew Black
Publisher
Neil Sumner

Contributors
Richard Ardagh
Grzegorz Piatek
Meirion Pritchard
Ellie Stathaki
Anna Tryc-Bromley

Wallpaper* ® is a
registered trademark
of IPC Media Limited

All prices are correct at
time of going to press,
but are subject to change.

PHAIDON

Phaidon Press Limited
Regent's Wharf
All Saints Street
London N1 9PA

Phaidon Press Inc
180 Varick Street
New York, NY 10014

Phaidon® is a registered
trademark of Phaidon
Press Limited

www.phaidon.com

First published 2007
© 2007 IPC Media Limited

ISBN 978 0 7148 4754 2

A CIP Catalogue record for
this book is available from
the British Library.

Printed in China

PHOTOGRAPHERS

Trevor Allen/Alamy
Kazimierz Dolny,
pp102-103

Nicolas Grospierre
Warsaw city view, inside
front cover
Warsaw University Library,
pp010-011
Palace of Culture and
Science, p012
Świętokrzyski Bridge, p013
Warsaw Central Station,
pp014-015
Residence Diana, p017
Le Régina, pp018-019
Polonia Palace Hotel, p022
InterContinental, p023
Café 6/12, p025
Wilanów Poster Museum,
pp026-027
Sense, pp028-029
Zachęta National Gallery
of Art, p030
Belvedere, p031
Foksal 19, p033
Kafka, p034, p035
U Kucharzy, p038
Czuły Barbarzyńca,
pp040-041
Qchnia Artystyczna, p043
Fabryka Trzciny,
pp050-051
Ania Kuczyńska, p055
Saska Kępa, p057
St Andrzeja Boboli church,
pp058-059
Warsaw School of
Economics, p062

Złote Tarasy, p063
Plac Wilsona metro station,
pp064-65
Metropolitan, pp066-067
Sejm, p068, p069
Royal Netherlands
Embassy, pp070-071
Magazyn Praga,
pp074-075
Wedel Chocolate
Parlour, p076
Zoom, pp078-079
Mielżyński, pp080-081
Galilu Neoperfumeria,
pp084-085
LAD Royal Weaving
Workshops, pp086-087
Akademia Wychowania
Fizycznego, pp090-091
Dr Irena Eris Cosmetic
Institute, p092
Buksza Polo Club, p093
Drapacz Chmur,
Katowice, p097

Look Galeria/Alamy
Silesian Library, Katowice,
pp098-099

Jochen Tack
Basketball, p089

**Detlef Westerkamp/
Ostkreuz**
Sopot, pp100-101

WARSAW
A COLOUR-CODED GUIDE TO THE HOT 'HOODS

WOLA
Office blocks are sprouting up as this industrial area morphs into the city's financial district

MOKOTÓW
The bars, cafés and restaurants of this enclave are popular with creative types

ŻOLIBORZ
A quiet modernist district that's characterised by wide streets, pretty parks and squares

POWIŚLE
Smart new developments are bringing a lively café culture to this once-rundown area

PRAGA
Artists are colonising this edgy zone, one of the few intact remnants of prewar Warsaw

STARE MIASTO/NOWE MIASTO
Warsaw's historic centre was levelled in WWII, but has been lovingly rebuilt, brick by brick

ŚRÓDMIEŚCIE
Immerse yourself in this district's brutal modernist architecture and buzzing nightlife

SASKA KĘPA
Embassies and expats inhabit the villas of this leafy, modernist neighbourhood

For a full description of each neighbourhood, see the Introduction.
Featured venues are colour-coded, according to the district in which they are located.